A Caricature of Marxism and Imperialist Economism

Workers of All Countries, Unite!

A Caricature of Marxism and Imperialist Economism

WILDSIDE PRESS

www.wildsidepress.com

PUBLISHERS' NOTE

This translation is taken from Volume 23 of V. I. Lenin's *Collected Works* in 45 volumes prepared by Progress Publishers, Moscow.

Contents

"No one can discredit revolutionary Social-Democracy as long as it does not discredit itself." That maxim always comes to mind, and must always be borne in mind, when any major theoretical or tactical proposition of Marxis mis victorious, or even placed on the order of the day, and when, *besides* outright and resolute opponents, it is assailed by friends who hopelessly discredit and disparage it and turn it into a caricature. That has happened time and again in the history of the Russian Social-Democratic movement. In the early nineties, the victory of Marxism in the revolutionary movement was attended by the emergence of a caricature of Marxism in the shape of Economism,[1] or "strikeism". The Iskrists[2] would not have been able to uphold the fundamentals of proletarian theory and policy, either against petty-bourgeois Narodism[3] or bourgeois liberalism, without long years of struggle against Economism. It was the same with Bolshevism, which triumphed in the mass labour movement in 1905 due, among other things, to correct application of the boycott of the tsarist Duma[4] slogan in the autumn of 1905, when the key battles of the Russian revolution were being fought. Bolshevism had to face—and overcome by struggle—another caricature in 1908-10, when Alexinsky and others noisily opposed participation in the Third Duma.[5]

It is the same today too. Recognition of the *present* war as imperialist and emphasis on *its* close connection with the imperialist era of capitalism encounters not only resolute opponents, but also irresolute friends, for whom the word "imperialism" has become all the rage. Having *memorised* the word, they are offering the workers hopelessly confused theories and reviving many of the old mistakes of the old Economism. Capitalism has triumphed—*therefore* there is no need to bother with political problems, the old Economists reasoned in 1894-1901, falling into rejection of the political struggle in Russia. Imperialism has triumphed—*therefore* there is no need to bother with the problems of political democracy, reason the present-day imperialist Economists. Kievsky's article,[6] printed above, merits attention as a sample of these sentiments, as one such caricature of Marxism, as the first attempt to provide anything like an integral literary exposition of the vacillation that has been apparent in certain circles of our Party abroad since early 1915.

If imperialist Economism were to spread among the Marxists, who in the present great crisis of socialism[7] have resolutely come out against social-chauvinism and for revolutionary internationalism, that would be a very grave blow to our trend—and to our Party. For it would discredit it from within, from its own ranks, would make it a vehicle of caricaturised Marxism. It is therefore necessary to thoroughly discuss at least the most important of Kievsky's numerous errors, regardless of how "uninteresting" this may be, and regardless of the fact, also, that all too often we shall have to tediously explain elementary truths which the thoughtful and attentive reader has learned and understood long since from our literature of 1914 and 1915.

We shall begin with the "central" point of Kievsky's disquisitions in order to immediately bring to the reader the very "substance" of this new trend of imperialist Economism.

1. The Marxist Attitude Towards War and "Defence of the Fatherland"

Kievsky is convinced, and wants to convince his reader, that he "disagrees" *only* with §9 of our Party Programme[8] dealing with national self-determination. He is very angry and tries to refute the charge that on the question of democracy he is departing from the fundamentals of Marxism *in general*, that he has "betrayed" (the angry quotation marks are Kievsky's) Marxism on basic issues. But the point is that the moment our author begins to discuss his allegedly partial disagreement on an individual issue, the moment he adduces his arguments, considerations, etc., he immediately reveals that he is deviating from Marxism all along the line. Take §b (Section 2) of his article. "This demand [i.e., national self-determination] directly [! !] leads to social-patriotism," our author proclaims, explaining that the "treasonous" slogan of fatherland defence follows "quite [!] logically [!] from the right of nations to self-determination".... In his opinion, self-determination implies "sanctioning the treason of the French and Belgian social-patriots, who are defending this independence [the national independence of France and Belgium] with arms in hand! They are *doing* what the supporters of 'self-determination' only advocate...." "Defence of the fatherland belongs to the arsenal of our worst enemies...." "We categorically refuse to understand how one can *simultaneously* be against defence of the fatherland and for self-determination, against the fatherland and for it."

That's Kievsky. He obviously has not understood our resolutions against the fatherland defence slogan in the present war. It is therefore necessary again to explain the meaning of what is so clearly set out in our resolutions.

The resolution our Party adopted at its Berne Conference[9] in March 1915, "On the Defence of the Fatherland Slogan", begins with the words: *"The present war is, in substance"....*

That the resolution deals with the *present* war could not have been put more plainly. The words "in substance" indicate that we must distinguish between the apparent and the real, between appearance and substance, between the word and the deed. The purpose of all talk about defence of the fatherland in this war is mendaciously to present as national the imperialist war of 1914-16, waged for the division of colonies, the plunder of foreign lands, etc. And to obviate even the slightest possibility of distorting our views, we added to the resolution a special paragraph on "*genuinely* national wars", which "took place *especially* (especially does not mean exclusively!) between 1789 and 1871".

The resolution explains that the "basis" of these "genuinely" national wars was a "long process of mass national movements, of a struggle against absolutism and feudalism, the overthrow of national oppression"....

Clear, it would seem. The present imperialist war stems from the general conditions of the imperialist era and is not accidental, not an exception, not a deviation from the general and typical. Talk of defence of the fatherland is therefore a deception of the people, for this war is *not* a national war. In a *genuinely* national war the words "defence of the fatherland" are *not* a deception and *we are not opposed to it.* Such (genuinely national) wars took place "especially" in 1789-1871, and our resolution, while not denying by a single word that they are possible now too, explains how we should distinguish a genuinely national from an imperialist war covered by deceptive national slogans. Specifically, in order to distinguish the two we must examine whether the "basis" of the war is a "long process of mass national movements", the "overthrow of national oppression".

The resolution on "pacifism" expressly states: "Social-Democrats cannot overlook the positive significance of revolutionary wars, i.e., not imperialist wars, but such as were conducted, for instance [note: "for instance"], between 1789 and 1871 with the aim of doing away with national oppression...." Could our 1915 Party resolution speak of the national wars waged from 1789 to 1871 and say that we do not deny the positive significance of such wars if they were not considered possible today too? Certainly not.

A commentary, or popular explanation, of our Party resolutions is given in the Lenin and Zinoviev pamphlet *Socialism and War.* It plainly states, on page 5, that "socialists have regarded wars 'for the defence of the fatherland', or 'defensive' wars, as legitimate, progressive and just" *only* in the sense of "overthrowing alien oppression". It cites an example: Persia against Russia, "*etc.*", and says: "These would be just, and defensive wars, irrespective of who would be the first to attack; any socialist would wish the oppressed, dependent and unequal states victory over the oppressor, slave-holding and predatory 'Great' Powers."

The pamphlet appeared in August 1915 and there are German and French translations. Kievsky is fully aware of its contents. And never, on no occasion, has he or anyone else challenged the resolution on the defence of the fatherland slogan, or the resolution on pacifism, or their interpretation in the pamphlet. Never, not once! We are therefore entitled to ask: are we slandering Kievsky when we say that he has absolutely failed to understand Marxism if, beginning with March 1915, he has not challenged our Party's views on the war, whereas now, in August 1916, in an article on self-determination, i.e., on a supposedly partial issue, he reveals an amazing lack of understanding of a *general* issue?

Kievsky says that the fatherland defence slogan is "treasonous". We can confidently assure him that *every* slogan is and always will be "treasonous" *for those* who mechanically repeat it without understanding its meaning, without giving it proper thought, *for those* who merely memorise the words without analysing their implications.

What, generally speaking, is "defence of the fatherland"? Is it a scientific concept relating to economics, politics, etc.? No. It is a much bandied about current expression, sometimes simply a philistine phrase, intended to *justify the war*. Nothing more. Absolutely nothing! The term "treasonous" can apply only in the sense that the philistine is capable of justifying *any* war by pleading "we are defending our fatherland", whereas Marxism, which does not degrade itself by stooping to the philistine's level, requires an historical analysis of each war in order to determine whether or not *that particular* war can be considered progressive, whether it serves the interests of democracy and the proletariat and, in *that sense*, is legitimate, just, etc.

The defence of the fatherland slogan is all too often unconscious philistine justification of war and reveals inability to analyse the meaning and implications of a particular war and see it in historical perspective.

Marxism makes that analysis and says: *if* the "substance" of a war is, *for example*, the overthrow of alien oppression (which was *especially* typical of Europe in 1789-1871), then such a war is progressive as far as the oppressed state or nation is concerned. *If*, however, the "substance" of a war is redivision of colonies, division of booty, plunder of foreign lands (and such is the war of 1914-16), then all talk of defending the fatherland is "sheer deception of the people."

How, then, can we disclose and define the "substance" of a war? War is the continuation of policy. Consequently, we must examine the policy pursued prior to the war, the policy that led to and brought about the war. If it was an imperialist policy, i.e., one designed to safeguard the interests of finance capital and rob and oppress colonies and foreign countries, then the war stemming from that policy is imperialist. If it was a national liberation policy, i.e., one expressive of the mass movement against national oppression, then the war stemming from that policy is a war of national liberation.

The philistine does not realise that war is "the continuation of policy", and consequently limits himself to the formula that "the enemy has attacked us", "the enemy has invaded my country", without stopping to think *what issues* are at stake in the war, *which* classes are waging it, and with *what* political objects. Kievsky stoops right down to the level of such a philistine when he declares that Belgium has been occupied by the Germans, and hence, from the point of view of self-determination, the "Belgian social-patriots are right", or: the Germans have occupied part of France, hence, "Guesde[10] can be satisfied", for 'what is involved is territory populated by his nation" (and not by an alien nation).

For the philistine the important thing is *where* the armies stand, who is winning *at the moment*. For the Marxist the important thing is *what issues* are at stake in *this* war, during which first one, then the other army may be on top.

What is the present war being fought over? The answer is given in our resolution (based on the *policy* the belligerent powers pursued for *decades* prior to the war). England, France and Russia are fighting to keep the colonies they have seized, to be able to rob Turkey, etc. Germany is fighting to take over these colonies and to be able herself to rob Turkey, etc. Let us suppose even that the Germans take Paris or St. Petersburg. Would that change the nature of the present war? Not at all. The Germans' purpose—and more important, the policy that would bring it to realisation if they were to win—is to seize the colonies, establish domination over Turkey, annex areas populated by other nations, for instance, Poland, etc. It is definitely not to bring the French or the Russians under foreign domination. The real essence of the present war is not national but imperialist. In other words, it is not being fought to enable one side to overthrow national oppression, which the other side is trying to maintain. It is a war between two groups of oppressors, between two freebooters over the division of their booty, over who shall rob Turkey and the colonies.

In short: a war *between* imperialist Great Powers (i. e., powers that oppress a whole number of nations and enmesh them in dependence on finance capital, etc.), or *in alliance* with the Great Powers, is an imperialist war. Such is the war of 1914-16. And in *this* war "defence of the fatherland" is a deception, and attempt to justify the war.

A war *against* imperialist, i.e., oppressing, powers by oppressed (for example, colonial) nations is a genuine national war. It is possible today too. "Defence of the fatherland" in a war waged by an oppressed nation against a foreign oppressor is not a deception. Socialists are *not* opposed to "defence of the fatherland" in *such* a war.

National self-determination is the same as the struggle for complete national liberation, for complete independence, against annexation, and socialists *cannot*—without ceasing to be socialists—reject *such* a struggle in whatever form, right down to an uprising or war.

Kievsky thinks he is arguing against Plekhanov[11]: it was Plekhanov who pointed to the link between self-determination and defence of the fatherland! Kievsky *believed* Plekhanov that the link was *really* of the kind Plekhanov made it out to be. And having believed him, Kievsky took fright and decided that he must reject self-determination so as not to fall into Plekhanov's conclusions. . . . There is great trust in Plekhanov, and great fright, but there is no trace of *thought* about the substance of Plekhanov's mistake!

The social-chauvinists plead self-determination in order to present this war as a national war. There is only one correct way of combating them: we must show that the war is being fought not to liberate nations, but to determine which of the great robbers will oppress *more* nations. To fall into negation of wars *really* waged for liberating nations is to present the worst possible caricature of Marxism. Plekhanov and the French social-chauvinists harp on the republic in France in order to justify its "defence" against the German monarchy. If we were to follow Kievsky's line of reasoning, we would have to oppose either the republic or a war *really* fought to preserve the republic!! The German social-chauvinists point to universal suffrage and compulsory primary education in their country to justify its "defence" against tsarism. If we were to follow Kievsky's line of reasoning, we would have to oppose either universal suffrage and compulsory primary education or a war *really* fought to safeguard political freedom against attempts to abolish it!

Up to the 1914-16 war Karl Kautsky[12] was a Marxist, and many of his major writings and statements will always remain models of Marxism. On August 26, 1910, he wrote in *Die Neue Zeit,* in reference to the imminent war:

> "In a war between Germany and England the issue is not democracy, but world domination, i.e., exploitation of the world. That is not an issue on which Social-Democrats can side with the exploiters of their nation" (*Neue Zeit, 28.* Jahrg., Bd. 2, S. 776).

There you have an excellent Marxist formulation, one that fully coincides with our own and fully exposes the *present-day* Kautsky, who has turned from Marxism to defence of social-chauvinism. It is a formulation (we shall have occasion to revert to it in other articles) that clearly brings out the principles underlying the Marxist attitude towards war. War is the continuation of policy. Hence, once there is a struggle for democracy, a war for democracy is *possible.* National self-determination is but one of the democratic demands and does not, in principle, differ from other democratic demands. "World domination" is, to put it briefly, the substance of imperialist policy, of which imperialist war is the continuation. Rejection of "defence of the fatherland" in a democratic war, *i.e.,* rejecting participation in such a war, is an absurdity that has nothing in common with Marxism. To embellish imperialist war by applying to it the concept of "defence of the fatherland", i.e., by presenting it as a democratic war, is to deceive the workers and side with the reactionary bourgeoisie.

2. "Our Understanding of the New Era"

The heading is Kievsky's. He constantly speaks of a "new era", but here, too, unfortunately his arguments are erroneous.

Our Party resolutions speak of the present war as stemming from the general conditions of the imperialist era. We give a correct Marxist definition of the relation between the "era" and the "present war": Marxism requires a concrete assessment of each separate war. To understand why an imperialist war, i.e., a war thoroughly reactionary and anti-democratic in its political implications, could, and inevitably did, break out between the Great Powers, many of whom stood at the head of the struggle for democracy in 1789-1871—to understand this we must understand the general conditions of the imperialist era, i.e., the transformation of capitalism in the advanced countries into imperialism.

Kievsky has flagrantly distorted the relation between the "era" and the "present war". In his reasoning, to consider the matter *concretely* means to examine the "era". That is precisely where he is wrong.

The era 1789-1871 was of special significance for Europe. That is irrefutable. We cannot understand a single national liberation war, and such wars were especially typical of that period, unless we understand the general conditions of the period. Does that mean that *all* wars of that period were national liberation wars? Certainly not. To hold that view is to reduce the whole thing to an absurdity and apply a ridiculous stereotype in place of a concrete analysis of each separate war. There were also colonial wars in 1789-1871, and wars between reactionary empires that oppressed many nations.

Advanced European (and American) capitalism has entered a new era of imperialism. Does it follow from that that the only imperialist wars are now possible? Any such contention would be absurd. It would reveal inability to distinguish a given concrete phenomenon from the sum total of variegated phenomena possible in a given era. An era is called an era precisely because it encompasses the sum total of variegated phenomena and wars, typical and untypical, big and small, some peculiar to advanced countries, others to backward countries. To brush aside these concrete questions by resorting to general phrases about the "era", as Kievsky does, is to abuse the very concept "era". And to prove that, we shall cite one example out of many. But first it should be noted that *one* group of Lefts, namely, the German *Internationale* group,[13] has advanced this manifestly erroneous proposition in § 5 of its theses, published in No. 3 of the *Bulletin of the Berne Executive Committee* (February 29, 1916): "National wars *are no longer possible* in the era of this unbridled imperialism." We analysed that statement in *Sbornik Sotsial-Demokrata.* Here we need merely note that though everyone who has followed the internationalist movement is long acquainted with this theoretical proposition (we opposed it way back in the spring of 1916 at the extended meeting of the Berne Executive Committee), *not a single group* has repeated or accepted it. And there is not a single word in the spirit of this or any similar proposition in Kievsky's article, written in August 1916.

That should be noted, and for the following reason: if this or a similar theoretical proposition were advanced, then we could speak of theoretical divergencies. But since *no* such proposition has been advanced, we are constrained to say: what we have is not a different interpretation of the concept "era", not a theoretical divergency, but merely a carelessly uttered phrase, merely abuse of the word "era".

Here is an example. Kievsky starts his article by asking: "Is not this (self-determination) the same as the right to receive free of charge 10,000 acres of land on Mars? The question can be answered only in the most concrete manner, only in context with the nature of the present era. The right of nations to self-determination is one thing in the era of the formation of national states, as the best form of developing the productive forces at their then existing level, but it is quite another thing now that this form, the national state, fetters the development of the productive forces. A vast distance separates the era of the establishment of capitalism and the national state from the era of the collapse of the national state and the eve of the collapse of capitalism itself. To discuss things in 'general' out of context with time and space, does not befit a Marxist".

There you have a sample of caricaturing the concept "imperialist era". And its caricature must be fought precisely because it is a new and important concept! What do we mean when we say that national states have become fetters, etc.? We have in mind the advanced capitalist countries, above all Germany, France, England, whose participation in the present war has been the chief factor in making it an imperialist war. In *these* countries, which hitherto have been in the van of mankind, particularly in 1789-1871, the process of forming national states has been consummated. In *these* countries the national movement is a thing of an irrevocable past, and it would be an absurd reactionary utopia to try to revive it. The national movement of the French, English, Germans has long been completed. In *these* countries history's next step is a different one: liberated nations have become transformed into oppressor nations, into nations of imperialist rapine, nations that are going through the "eve of the collapse of capitalism".

But what of other nations?

Kievsky repeats, like a rule learned by rote, that Marxists should approach things "concretely", but he does *not* apply that rule. In our theses[14], on the other hand, we deliberately gave an example of a concrete approach, and Kievsky did not wish to point out our mistake, if he found one.

Our theses (§ 6) state that to be concrete not less than *three* different types of countries must be distinguished when dealing with self-determination. (It was clearly impossible to discuss each separate country in general theses.) First type: the advanced countries of Western Europe (and America), where the national movement is a thing of the *past*. Second type: Eastern Europe, where it is a thing of the *present*. Third type: semi-colonies and colonies, where it is largely a thing of the *future*.

Is this correct or not? *This* is what Kievsky should have levelled his criticism at. But he does not see the *essence* of the theoretical problems! He fails to see that unless he refutes the above-mentioned proposition (in § 6) of our theses—and it cannot be refuted because it is correct—his disquisitions about the "era" resemble a man brandishing his sword but striking no blows.

> "In contrast to V. Ilyin's[15] opinion," he writes at the end of his article, "we assume that for the majority [!] of Western [!] countries the national problem has not been settled. . . ."

And so, the national movements of the French, Spaniards, English, Dutch, Germans and Italians were not consummated in the seventeenth, eighteenth and nineteenth centuries, and earlier? At the beginning of the article the concept "era of imperialism" is distorted to make it appear that the national movement has been consummated in general, and not only in the advanced Western countries. At the end of the same article the "national problem" is declared "not settled" in *precisely* the Western countries!! Is that not a muddle?

In the Western countries the national movement is a thing of the distant past. In England, France, Germany, etc., the "fatherland" is a dead letter, it has played its historical role, *i.e.*, the national movement cannot yield here anything progressive, anything that will elevate new masses to a new economic and political life. History's next step here is not transition from feudalism or from patriarchal savagery to national progress, to a cultured and politically free fatherland, but transition from a "fatherland" that has outlived its day, that is capitalistically overripe, to socialism.

The position is different in Eastern Europe. As far as the Ukrainians and Byelorussians, for instance, are concerned, only a Martian dreamer could deny that the national movement has not yet been consummated there, that the awakening of the masses to the full use of their mother tongue and literature (and this is an absolute condition and concomitant of the full development of capitalism, of the full penetration of exchange to the very last peasant family) is *still* going on there. The "fatherland" is historically not *yet* quite a dead letter there. There the "defence of the fatherland" can *still* be defence of democracy, of one's native language, of political liberty against oppressor nations, against medievalism, whereas the

English, French, Germans and Italians lie when they speak of defending their fatherland in the present war, because actually what they are defending is *not* their native language, *not* their right to national development, but their rights as slave-holders, their colonies, the foreign "spheres of influence" of their finance capital, etc.

In the semi-colonies and colonies the national movement is, historically, still younger than in Eastern Europe.

What do the words "advanced countries" and imperialist era refer to? In *what* lies the "special" position of Russia (heading of § e in the second chapter of Kievsky's article), and not only Russia? *Where* is the national liberation movement a false phrase and *where* is it a living and progressive reality? Kievsky reveals no understanding on any of these points.

3. What Is Economic Analysis?

Central to all the disquisitions of the self-determination opponents is the claim that it is generally "unachievable" under capitalism or imperialism. The word "unachievable" is frequently used in widely different and inaccurately defined meanings. That is why in our theses we insisted on what is essential in any theoretical discussion: an explanation of what is meant by "unachievable". Nor did we confine ourselves to that. We tried to give such an explanation. *All* democratic demands are "unachievable" under imperialism in the sense that politically they are hard to achieve or totally unachievable without a series of revolutions.

It is fundamentally wrong, however, to maintain that self-determination is unachievable in the economic sense.

That has been our contention. It is the pivotal point of our theoretical differences, a question to which our opponents in any serious discussion should have paid due attention.

But just see how Kievsky treats the question.

He definitely rejects unachievable as meaning "hard to achieve" politically. He gives a direct answer in the sense of economic unachievability.

"Does this mean," Kievsky writes, "that self-determination under imperialism is just as unachievable as labour money under commodity production?" And he replies: "Yes, it means exactly that. For what we are discussing is the logical contradiction between two social categories: 'imperialism' and 'self-determination of nations', the same logical contradiction as that between two other categories: labour money and commodity production. Imperialism is the negation of self-determination, and no magician can reconcile the two."

Frightening as is the angry word "magician" Kievsky hurls at us, we must nevertheless point out that he simply fails to understand what economic analysis implies. There should be no "logical contradiction"—providing, of course, that there is proper logical thinking —*either* in an economic *or* political analysis. Hence, to plead a "logical contradiction" *in general* when what we are discussing is economic and *not* political analysis, is completely irrelevant. *Both* economic and political phenomena come within "social categories". Consequently, having first replied directly and definitely: "Yes, it means exactly that" (i.e., self-determination is *just as* unachievable as labour money under commodity production), Kievsky dismisses the whole matter by beating about the bush, without offering any economic analysis.

How do we prove that labour money is unachievable under commodity production? By economic analysis. And economic analysis, like every other, rules out "logical contradictions", takes economic and *only* economic categories (and not "social categories" in general) and from them concludes that labour money is unachievable. In the first chapter of *Capital* there is no mention whatever of politics, or political forms, or "social categories": the analysis applies *only* to economic phenomena, commodity exchange, its development. Economic analysis shows—needless to say, through "logical" arguments—that under commodity production labour money is unachievable.

Kievsky does not even attempt anything approximating an economic analysis! He *confuses* the economic substance of imperialism with its political tendencies, as is obvious from the very first phrase of the very first paragraph of his article. Here is that phrase:

"Industrial capital is the synthesis of pre-capitalist production and merchant-usurer capital. Usurer capital becomes the servant of industrial capital. Then capitalism subjects the various forms of capital and there emerges its highest, unified type—finance capital. The whole era can therefore be designated as the era of finance capital of which imperialism is the corresponding foreign-policy system."

Economically, that definition is absolutely worthless: instead of precise economic categories we get mere phrases. However, it is impossible to dwell on that now. The important thing is that Kievsky proclaims imperialism to be a "foreign-policy system".

First, this is, essentially, a wrong repetition of Kautsky's wrong idea.

Second, it is a purely political, and only political, definition of imperialism. By defining imperialism as a "system of policy" Kievsky wants to avoid the *economic* analysis he promised to give when he declared that self-determination was "*just as*" unachievable, i.e., economically unachievable, under imperialism as labour money under commodity production!*

In his controversy with the Lefts, Kautsky declared that imperialism was "merely a system of foreign *policy*" (namely, annexation), and that it would be wrong to describe as imperialism a definite economic stage, or level, in the development of capitalism.

Kautsky is wrong. Of course, it is not proper to argue about words. You cannot prohibit the use of the "word" imperialism in this sense or any other. But if you want to conduct a discussion you must define your terms precisely.

Economically, imperialism (or the "era" of finance capital—it is not a matter of words) is the highest stage in the development of capitalism, one in which production has assumed such big, immense proportions that *free competition gives way to monopoly*. That is the *economic* essence of imperialism. Monopoly manifests itself in trusts, syndicates, etc., in the omnipotence of the giant banks, in

---

* Is Kievsky aware of the impolite word Marx used in reference to such "logical methods"? *Without applying* this impolite term to Kievsky, we nevertheless are obliged to remark that Marx described such methods as "fraudulent": arbitrarily inserting precisely what is at issue, precisely what has to be proved, in *defining* a concept.

We repeat, we do *not* apply Marx's impolite expression to Kievsky. We merely disclose the source of his mistake. (In the manuscript this passage is crossed out.—*Ed.*)

the buying up of raw material sources, etc., in the concentration of banking capital, etc. Everything hinges on economic monopoly.

The political superstructure of this new economy, of monopoly capitalism (imperialism is monopoly capitalism) is the change *from* democracy *to* political reaction. Democracy corresponds to free competition. Political reaction corresponds to monopoly. "Finance capital strives for domination, not freedom," Rudolf Hilferding rightly remarks in his *Finance Capital.*

It is fundamentally wrong, un-Marxist and unscientific, to single out "foreign policy" from policy in general, let alone counterpose foreign policy to home policy. Both in foreign and home policy imperialism strives towards violations of democracy, towards reaction. In this sense imperialism is indisputably the "negation" of *democracy in general*, of *all democracy,* and not just of *one* of its demands, national self-determination.

Being a "negation" of democracy in general, imperialism is *also* a "negation" of democracy in the national question (i.e., national self-determination): it seeks to violate democracy. The achievement of democracy is, in the same sense, and to the same degree, harder under imperialism (compared with pre-monopoly capitalism), as the achievement of a republic, a militia, popular election of officials, etc. There can be no talk of democracy being "economically" unachievable.

Kievsky was probably led astray here by the fact (besides his general lack of understanding of the requirements of economic analysis) that the philistine regards annexation (i.e., acquisition of foreign territories against the will of their people, i.e., violation of self-determination) as equivalent to the "spread" (expansion) of finance capital to a larger economic territory.

But theoretical problems should not be approached from philistine conceptions.

Economically, imperialism is monopoly capitalism. To acquire full monopoly, all competition must be eliminated, and not only on the home market (of the given state), but also on foreign markets, in the whole world. Is it *economically* possible, "in the era of finance capital", to eliminate competition even in a foreign state? Certainly it is. It is done through a rival's financial dependence and acquisition of his sources of raw materials and eventually of all his enterprises.

The American trusts are the supreme expression of the economics of imperialism or monopoly capitalism. They do not confine themselves to economic means of eliminating rivals, but constantly resort to political, even criminal, methods. It would be the greatest mistake, however, to believe that the trusts cannot establish their monopoly by purely economic methods. Reality provides ample proof that this is "achievable": the trusts undermine their rivals' credit through the banks (the owners of the trusts become the owners of the banks: buying up shares); their supply of materials (the owners of the trusts become the owners of the railways: buying up shares); for a certain time the trusts sell below cost, spending millions on this in order to ruin competitor and then *buy up* his enterprises, his sources of raw materials (mines, land, etc.).

There you have a purely economic analysis of the power of the trusts and their expansion. There you have the purely economic path to expansion: *buying up* mills and factories, sources of raw materials.

Big finance capital of one country can always buy up competitors in another, politically independent country and constantly does so. Economically, this is fully achievable. Economic "annexation" is *fully* "achievable" without political annexation and is widely practised. In the literature on imperialism you will constantly come across indications that Argentina, for example, is in reality a "trade colony" of Britain, or that Portugal is in reality a "vassal" of Britain, etc. And that is actually so: economic dependence upon British banks, indebtedness to Britain, British acquisition of their railways, mines, land, etc., enable Britain to "annex" these countries economically without violating their political independence.

National self-determination means political independence. Imperialism seeks to violate such independence because political annexation often makes economic annexation easier, cheaper (easier to bribe officials, secure concessions, put through advantageous legislation, etc.), more convenient, less troublesome—just as imperialism seeks to replace democracy generally by oligarchy. But to speak of the *economic* "unachievability" of self-determination under imperialism is sheer nonsense.

Kievsky gets round the theoretical difficulties by a very simple and superficial dodge, known in German as "*burschikose*" phraseology, i.e., primitive, crude phrases heard (and quite naturally) at student binges. Here is an example:

> "Universal suffrage," he writes, "the eight-hour day and even the republic are *logically* compatible with imperialism, though imperialism far from smiles [!!] on them and their achievement is therefore extremely difficult."

We would have absolutely no objections to the *burschikose* statement that imperialism far from "smiles" on the republic—a frivolous word can sometimes lend colour to a scientific polemic—if in this polemic on a serious issue we were given, *in addition*, an economic and political analysis of the concepts involved. With Kievsky, however, the *burschikose* phrase does duty for such an analysis or serves to conceal lack of it.

What can this mean: "Imperialism far from smiles on the republic"? And why?

The republic is one possible form of the political superstructure of capitalist society, and, moreover, under present-day conditions the most democratic form. To say that imperialism does not "smile" on the republic is to say that there is a contradiction between imperialism and democracy. It may very well be that Kievsky does not "smile" or even "far from smiles" on this conclusion. Nevertheless it is irrefutable.

To continue. What is the nature of this contradiction between imperialism and democracy? Is it a logical or illogical contradiction? Kievsky uses the word "logical" without stopping to think and therefore does not notice that in this particular case it serves to *conceal* (both from the reader's and author's eyes and mind) the *very question* he sets out to discuss! That question is the relation of economics to politics: the relation of economic conditions and the economic content of imperialism to a certain political form. To say that every "contradiction" revealed in human discussion is a logical contradiction is meaningless tautology. And with the aid of this tautology Kievsky evades the *substance* of the question: Is it a "logical" contradiction between two *economic* phenomena or propositions (1)? Or two *political* phenomena or propositions (2)? Or *economic* and *political* phenomena or propositions (3)?

For that is the heart of the matter, once we are discussing economic unachievability or achievability under one or another political form!

Had Kievsky not evaded the heart of the matter, he would probably have realised that the contradiction between imperialism and the republic is a contradiction between the economics of latter-day capitalism (namely, monopoly capitalism) and political democracy in general. For Kievsky will never prove that any major and fundamental democratic measure (popular election of officials or officers, complete freedom of association and assembly, etc.) is less contradictory to imperialism (or, if you like, more "smiled" upon) than the republic.

What we have, then, is the proposition *we* advanced in our theses: imperialism contradicts, "logically" contradicts, *all* political democracy *in general.* Kievsky does not "smile" on this proposition for it demolishes all his illogical constructions. But what can we do about it? Are we to accept a method that is supposed to refute certain propositions, but instead secretly advances them by using such expressions as "imperialism far from smiles on the republic"?

Further. Why does imperialism far from smile on the republic? And how does imperialism "combine" its economics with the republic?

Kievsky has given no thought to that. We would remind him of the following words of Engels in reference to the democratic republic. Can wealth dominate under this form of government? The question concerns the "contradiction" between economics and politics.

Engels replies: "The democratic republic officially knows nothing any more of property distinctions [between citizens]. In it, wealth exercises its power indirectly, but all the more surely. On the one hand, in the form of the direct corruption of officials, of which America provides the classical example; on the other hand, in the form of an alliance between government and stock exchange. . . ."[16]

There you have an excellent example of economic analysis on the question of the "achievability" of democracy under capitalism. And the "achievability" of self-determination under imperialism is part of that question.

The democratic republic "logically" contradicts capitalism, because "officially" it puts the rich and the poor on an equal footing. That is a contradiction between the economic system and the political superstructure. There is the same contradiction between imperialism and the republic, deepened or aggravated by the fact that the change-over from free competition to monopoly makes the realisation of political freedoms even more "difficult".

How, then, is capitalism reconciled with democracy? By indirect implementation of the omnipotence of capital. There are two economic means for that: (1) direct bribery; (2) alliance of government and stock exchange. (That is stated in our theses—under a bourgeois system finance capital "can freely bribe and buy any government and any official".)

Once we have the dominance of commodity production, of the bourgeoisie, of the power of money—bribery (direct or through the stock exchange) is "achievable" under any form of government and under any kind of democracy.

What, it can be asked, is altered in this respect when capitalism gives way to imperialism, i.e., when pre-monopoly capitalism is replaced by monopoly capitalism?

Only that the power of the stock exchange increases. For finance capital is industrial capital at its highest, monopoly level which has merged with banking capital. The big banks merge with and absorb the stock exchange. (The literature on imperialism speaks of the declining role of the stock exchange, but only in the sense that every giant bank is itself virtually a stock exchange).

Further. If "wealth" in general is fully capable of achieving domination over any democratic republic by bribery and through the stock exchange, then how can Kievsky maintain, without lapsing into a very curious "logical contradiction", that the immense wealth of the trusts and the banks, which have thousands of millions at their command, cannot "achieve" the domination of finance capital over a foreign, i.e., politically independent, republic??

Well? Bribery of officials is "unachievable" in a foreign state? Or the "alliance of government and stock exchange" applies only to one's own government?

* * *

The reader will already have seen that it requires roughly ten pages of print to untangle and popularly explain ten lines of confusion. We cannot examine every one of Kievsky's arguments in the same detail. And there is not a single one that is not confused. Nor is there really any need for this once the main arguments have been examined. The rest will be dealt with briefly.

4. The Example of Norway

Norway "achieved" the supposedly unachievable right to self-determination in 1905, in the era of the most rampant imperialism. It is therefore not only absurd, but ludicrous, from the theoretical standpoint, to speak of "unachievability".

Kievsky wants to refute that by angrily calling us "rationalists". (What has that to do with it? The nationalist confines himself to purely abstract disquisitions, while we have pointed to a very concrete fact! But perhaps Kievsky is using the foreign word "rationalist" in the same . . . how to put it more mildly?. . . in the same "unhappy" manner he used the word "extractive" at the beginning of his article, when he presented his arguments "in extractive form"?)

Kievsky reproaches us. For us, he says, "the important thing is the appearance of phenomena rather than the real substance". Well, let us examine the real substance.

His refutation begins with this example: enactment of a law against trusts does not prove that their prohibition is unachievable. True enough. But the example is an unhappy one, for it militates *against* Kievsky. Laws are political measures, politics. No political measure can prohibit economic phenomena. Whatever political form Poland adopts, whether she be part of tsarist Russia or Germany, or an autonomous region, or a politically independent state, there is no prohibiting or repealing her dependence on the finance capital of the imperialist powers, or preventing that capital from buying up the shares of her industries.

The independence Norway "achieved" in 1905 was only political. It could not affect its economic dependence, nor was this the intention. That is exactly the point made in our theses. We indicated that self-determination concerns only politics, and it would therefore be wrong even to raise the question of its economic unachievability. But here is Kievsky "refuting" this by citing an example of political bans being powerless against the economy! What a "refutation"!

To proceed.

"One or even many instances of small-scale industry prevailing over large-scale industry is not sufficient to refute Marx's correct proposition that the general development of capitalism is attended by the concentration and centralisation of production."

Again, the argument is based on an unfortunate *example*, chosen to divert the attention (of the reader and the author) from the substance of the issue.

We maintain that it would be wrong to speak of the economic unachievability of self-determination in the same sense as we speak of the unachievability of labour money under capitalism. Not a single "example" of *such* achievability can be cited. Kievsky tacitly admits we are correct on this point when he shifts to *another* interpretation of "unachievability".

Why does he not do so directly? Why does he not openly and precisely formulate *his* proposition: "self-determination, while unachievable in the sense that it is economically impossible under capitalism, contradicts development and is therefore either reactionary or merely an exception"?

He does not do so because a clear formulation of this counter-proposition would immediately expose its author, and he therefore tries to conceal it.

The law of economic concentration, of the victory of large-scale production over small, is recognised in our own and the Erfurt programmes.[17] Kievsky conceals the fact that nowhere is the law of political or state concentration recognised. If it were the same kind of law—if there were such a law—then why should not Kievsky formulate it and suggest that it be added to our programme? Is it right for him to leave us with a bad, incomplete programme, considering that he has discovered this new law of state concentration, which is of practical significance since it would rid our programme of erroneous conclusions?

Kievsky does not formulate that law, does not suggest that it be added to our programme, because he has the hazy feeling that if he did he would be making himself a laughing-stock. Everyone would laugh at this amusing imperialist Economism if it were expressed openly and if, parallel with the law that small-scale production is ousted by large-scale production, there were presented another "*law*" (connected with the first or existing side by side with it) of small states being ousted by big ones!

To explain this we shall put only one question to Kievsky: Why is it that economists (without quotation marks) do *not* speak of the "disintegration" of the modern trusts or big banks? Or of the possibility and achievability of such disintegration? Why is it that even the "imperialist Economist" (in quotation marks) is obliged to admit that the disintegration of big states is both possible and achievable, and not only in general, but, for example, the secession of "small nationalities" (please note!) from Russia (§ e, Chapter II of Kievsky's article)?

Lastly, to show even more clearly the lengths to which our author goes, and to warn him, let us note the following: We all accept the law of large-scale production ousting small-scale production, but no one is afraid to describe a specific "instance" of "small-scale industry prevailing over large-scale industry" as a reactionary phenomenon. *No* opponent of self-determination has yet ventured to describe as reactionary Norway's secession from Sweden, though we raised the question in our literature as early as 1914.

Large-scale production is unachievable if, for instance, hand-worked machines remain. The idea of a mechanical factory "disintegrating" into handicrafts production is utterly absurd. The imperialist tendency towards big empires is fully achievable, and in practice is often achieved, in the form of an imperialist alliance of sovereign and independent—politically independent—states. Such an alliance is possible and is encountered not only in the form of an economic merger of the finance capital of two countries, but also in the form of military "co-operation" in an imperialist war. National struggle, national insurrection, national secession are fully "achievable" and are met with in practice *under* imperialism. They are even more pronounced, for imperialism does not halt the development of capitalism and the growth of democratic tendencies among the mass of the population. On the contrary, it *accentuates* the antagonism between their democratic aspirations and the anti-democratic tendency of the trusts.

It is only from the point of view of imperialist Economism, i.e., caricaturised Marxism, that one can ignore, for instance, this specific aspect of imperialist policy: on the one hand, the present imperialist war offers examples of how the force of financial ties and economic interests draws a small, politically independent state into the struggle of the Great Powers (Britain and Portugal). On the other hand, the violation of democracy with regard to small nations, much weaker (both economically and politically) than their imperialist "patrons", leads either to revolt (Ireland) or to defection of whole regiments to the enemy (the Czechs). In this situation it is not only "achievable", from the point of view of finance capital, but *sometimes* even *profitable* for the trusts, for *their* imperialist policy, for *their* imperialist war, to allow *individual* small nations as much democratic freedom as they can, right down to political independence, so as not to risk damaging their "own" military operations. To overlook the peculiarity of political and strategic relationships and to repeat indiscriminately a word learned by rote, "imperialism", is anything but Marxism.

On Norway, Kievsky tells us, firstly, that she "had always been an independent state". That is not true and can only be explained by the author's *burschikose* carelessness and his disregard of political issues. Norway was *not* an independent state prior to 1905, though she enjoyed a very large measure of autonomy. Sweden recognised Norway's political independence only *after* her secession. If Norway "had always been an independent state", then the Swedish Government would not have informed the other powers, on October 26, 1905, that it recognised Norway's independence.

Secondly, Kievsky cites a number of statements to prove that Norway looked to the West, and Sweden to the East, that in one country mainly British, and in the other German, finance capital was "at work", etc. From this he draws the triumphant conclusion: "This example [Norway] neatly fits into our pattern."

There you have a sample of the logic of imperialist Economism! Our theses point out that finance capital can dominate in "any", "even independent country", and all the arguments about self-determination being "unachievable" from the point of view of finance capital are therefore sheer confusion. We are given data *confirming* our proposition about the part foreign finance capital played in Norway *before* and *after* her secession. And these data are supposed to *refute* our proposition!

Dilating on finance capital in order to *disregard* political issues—is that the way to discuss politics?

No. Political issues do not disappear because of Economism's faulty logic. British finance capital was "at work" in Norway before and after secession. German finance capital was "at work" in Poland prior to her secession from Russia and will continue to "work" there *no matter* what political status Poland enjoys. That is so elementary that it is embarrassing to have to repeat it. But what can one do if the ABC is forgotten?

Does this dispense with the political question of Norway's status? With her having been part of Sweden? With the attitude of the workers when the secession issue arose?

Kievsky evades these questions because they hit hard at the Economists. But these questions were posed, and are posed, by life itself. Life itself posed the question: Could a Swedish worker who did not recognise Norway's right to secession remain a member of the Social-Democratic Party? *He could not.*

The Swedish aristocrats wanted a war against Norway, and so did the clericals. That fact does not disappear because Kievsky has "forgotten" to read about it in the history of the Norwegian people. The Swedish worker could, while remaining a Social-Democrat, urge the Norwegians to vote against secession (the Norwegian referendum on secession, held on August 13, 1905, resulted in 368, 200 votes for secession and 184 against, with about 80 per cent of the electorate taking part). But the Swedish worker who, like the Swedish aristocracy and bourgeoisie, would deny the Norwegians the right to decide this question themselves, without the Swedes and irrespective of their will, would have been a *social-chauvinist* and *a miscreant the Social-Democratic Party could not tolerate in its ranks.*

That is how §9 of our Party Programme should be applied. But our imperialist Economist tries to *jump over* this clause. You cannot jump over it, gentlemen, without falling into the embrace of chauvinism!

And what of the Norwegian worker? Was it his duty, from the internationalist point of view, to vote *for* secession? Certainly not. He could have voted against secession and remained a Social-Democrat. He would have been betraying his duty as a member of the Social-Democratic Party only if he had proffered a helping hand to a Black Hundred Swedish worker opposed to Norway's *freedom* of secession.

Some people refuse to see this elementary difference in the position of the Norwegian and Swedish worker. But they expose themselves when they *evade* this most concrete of political questions, which we squarely put to them. They remain silent, try to wriggle out and in that way surrender their position.

To prove that the "Norwegian" issue can arise in Russia, we deliberately advanced this proposition: in circumstances of a *purely* military and strategic nature a separate Polish state is fully achievable even *now.* Kievsky wants to "discuss" that—and remains silent!

Let us add this: Finland too, out of *purely* military and strategic considerations, and given a certain outcome of the *present* imperialist war (for instance, Sweden joining the Germans and the latter's semi-victory), *can* become a separate state without undermining the "achievability" of even a single operation of finance capital, without making "unachievable" the buying up of Finnish railway and industrial shares.*

Kievsky seeks salvation from unpleasant political issues in an amazing phrase which is amazingly characteristic of all his "arguments": "At any moment ... [that is literally what he says at the end of §c, Chapter I] the Sword of Damocles can strike and put an end to the existence of an 'independent' workshop" (a "hint" at little Sweden and Norway).

That, presumably, is genuine Marxism: a separate Norwegian state, whose secession from Sweden the *Swedish* Government described as a "revolutionary measure", has been in existence only some ten years. Is there any point in examining the *political* issues that follow from this if we have read Hilferding's *Finance Capital* and "understood" it in the sense that "at any moment"—if we are to exaggerate then let's go the whole hog!—a small state might vanish? Is there any point in drawing attention to the fact that we have perverted Marxism into Economism, and that we have turned our policy into a rehash of the speeches of case-hardened Russian chauvinists?

What a mistake the Russian workers must have made in 1905 in seeking a republic: finance capital had already been mobilised against it in France, England, etc., and "at any moment" the "Sword of Damocles" could have struck it down, if it had ever come into being!

---

* Given one outcome of the present war, the formation of new states in Europe (Polish, Finnish, etc.) is fully "achievable" without in any way disturbing the conditions for the development of imperialism and its power. On the contrary, this would *increase* the influence, contacts and pressure of finance capital. But given another outcome, the formation of new states in Hungary, Czechia, etc., is *likewise* "achievable". The British imperialists are already planning this second outcome in anticipation of their victory. The imperialist era does not destroy either the striving for national political independence or its "achievability" *within the bounds* of world imperialist relationships. *Outside* these bounds, however, a republican Russia, or in general any major democratic transformations anywhere else in the world are "unachievable" without a series of revolutions and are unstable without socialism. Kievsky has wholly and completely failed to understand the relation of imperialism to democracy.

* * *

"The demand for national self-determination is not . . . utopian in the minimum programme: it does not contradict social development, inasmuch as its achievement would not halt that development." That passage from Martov[18] is challenged by Kievsky in the section in which he cites the "statements" about Norway. They *prove,* again and again, the generally known fact that Norway's "self-determination" and secession *did not halt either* the development of finance capital generally, *or* expansion of its operation in particular, *or* the buying up of Norway by the English!

There have been Bolsheviks among us, Alexinsky in 1908-10, for instance, who argued with Martov *precisely at a time* when Martov was right! God save us from such "allies"!

5. "Monism and Dualism"

Reproaching us for "interpreting the demand dualistically", P. Kievsky writes:

> "Monistic *action* of the International is replaced by dualistic *propaganda.*"

That sounds quite Marxist and materialistic: monistic action is contrasted to "dualistic" propaganda. Unfortunately, closer examination reveals that it is *verbal* "monism", like the "monism" of Dühring. "If I include a shoe brush in the *unity* mammals," Engels wrote exposing Dühring's "monism", "this does not help it to get mammary glands."[19]

This means that only such things, qualities, phenomena and actions that are *a unity* in objective reality can be *declared* "a unity". It is this "*detail*" that our author overlooks!

He thinks we are "dualists", first, because what we demand, primarily, of the workers of the oppressed nations—this refers to the national question only—*differs* from what we demand of the workers of the oppressor nations.

To determine whether P. Kievsky's "monism" is the same as Dühring's, let us examine *objective realities.*

Is the *actual* condition of the workers in the oppressor and in the oppressed nations the same, from the standpoint of the national question?

No, it is not the same.

(1) *Economically,* the difference is that section of the working class in the oppressor nations receive crumbs from the *superprofits* the bourgeoisie of these nations obtains by extra exploitation of the workers of the oppressed nations. Besides, economic statistics show that here a *larger* percentage of the workers become "straw bosses" than is the case in the oppressed nations, a *larger* percentage rise to the labour *aristocracy.** That is a fact. To a *certain degree* the workers of the oppressor nations are partners of *their own* bourgeoisie in plundering the workers (and the mass of the population) of the oppressed nations.

(2) *Politically,* the difference is that, compared with the workers of the oppressed nations, they occupy a *privileged* position in many spheres of political life.

(3) *Ideologically,* or spiritually, the difference is that they are taught, at school and in life, disdain and contempt for the workers of the oppressed nations. This has been *experienced,* for example, by every Great Russian who has been brought up or who has lived among Great Russians.

Thus, *all along the line* there are differences in objective reality, i.e., "dualism" in the objective world that is independent of the will and consciousness of individuals.

That being so, how are we to regard P. Kievsky's assertion about the "monistic action of the International"?

It is a hollow, high-sounding phrase, no more.

In *real life* the International is composed of workers *divided* into oppressor and oppressed nations. *If* its action is *to be monistic,* its propaganda must *not* be the same for both. That is how we should regard the matter in the light of real (not Dühringian) "monism", Marxist materialism.

An example? We cited the example of Norway (in the legal press over two years ago!), and no one has challenged it. In this concrete case taken from life, the *action* of

* See, for instance, Hourwich's book on immigration and the condition of the working class in America, *Immigration and Labor.* —*Ed.*

the Norwegian and Swedish workers was "monistic", unified, internationalist *only* because and insofar as the Swedish workers *unconditionally* championed Norway's freedom to secede, while the Norwegian workers raised the question of secession only *conditionally*. Had the Swedish workers not supported Norway's freedom of secession *unconditionally*, they would have been *chauvinists*, accomplices of the chauvinist Swedish landlords, who wanted to "keep" Norway by force, by war. Had the Norwegian workers *not* raised the question of secession *conditionally*, i.e., allowing even Social-Democratic Party members to conduct propaganda and vote against secession, they would have failed in their internationalist duty and would have sunk to narrow, *bourgeois* Norwegian nationalism. Why? Because the secession was being effected by the *bourgeoisie*, not by the proletariat! Because the Norwegian bourgeoisie, (as every other) *always* strives to drive a wedge between the workers of its own and an "alien" country! Because for the class-conscious workers every democratic demand (including self-determination) is *subordinated* to the supreme interests of socialism. For example, if Norway's secession from Sweden had created the certainty or probability of war between Britain and Germany, the Norwegian workers, *for that reason alone*, would have had to oppose secession. The Swedish workers would have had the right and the opportunity, without ceasing to be socialists, to agitate against secession, but *only* if they had waged a systematic, consistent and constant struggle *against* the Swedish Government for Norway's *freedom* to secede. Otherwise the Norwegian workers and people *would not*, and *could not*, accept the advice of the Swedish workers as sincere.

The trouble with the opponents of self-determination is that they confine themselves to lifeless abstractions, *fearing* to analyse to the end a single concrete real-life instance. Our concrete statement in the theses that a new Polish state is quite "achievable" *now*, given a definite combination of purely military, strategic conditions, has not been challenged either by the Poles or by P. Kievsky. But no one wanted to *ponder* the conclusions that follow from this tacit admission that we were right. And what follows, obviously, is that internationalist propaganda *cannot* be the same for the Russians and the Poles if it is to educate both for "monistic action". The Great-Russian (and German) worker is in duty bound unconditionally to insist on Poland's freedom to secede; otherwise he will, *in fact, now,* be the lackey of Nicholas II or Hindenburg. The Polish worker *could* insist on secession *only* conditionally, because to speculate (as do the Fracy[20]) on the victory of one or the other imperialist bourgeoisie is tantamount to becoming *its* lackey.

Failure to understand this difference, which is a prerequisite for "monistic action" of the International, is about the same as failing to understand why "monistic action" against the tsarist army near Moscow, say, requires that the revolutionary forces march west from Nizhni-Novgorod and east from Smolensk.

* * *

Second, our new exponent of Dühringian monism reproaches us for not striving to achieve "the closest organisational unity of the various national sections of the International" in the event of a social revolution.

Under socialism, P. Kievsky writes, self-determination becomes superfluous, since the state itself ceases to exist. That is meant as an argument against us! But in our theses we clearly and definitely say, in *three* lines, the last three lines of section one, that "democracy, too, is a form of state which must disappear when the state disappears". It is precisely this truism that P. Kievsky repeats—to "refute" us, of course!—on *several pages* of his §r (Chapter I), and repeats it in a *distorted way*. "We picture to ourselves," he writes, "and have always pictured the socialist system as a strictly democratic [!!?], centralised system of economy in which the state, as the apparatus for the domination of one part of the population over the other, disappears." This is confusion, because democracy *too* is domination "of one part of the population over the other"; it *too* is a form of state. Our author obviously does not understand what is meant by the *withering away* of the state after the victory of socialism and what this process requires.

The main point, however, is his "objections" regarding the era of the social revolution. He calls us "talmudists of self-determination"—what a frightening epithet—and adds: "We picture this process [the social revolution] as the united action of the proletarians of all [!] countries, who wipe out the frontiers of the bourgeois [!] state, who tear down the frontier posts [in addition to "wiping out the frontiers"?], who blow up [!] national unity and establish class unity."

The wrath of this stern judge of the "talmudists" notwithstanding, we must say: there are many words here, but no "ideas".

The social revolution cannot be the united action of the proletarians of *all* countries for the simple reason that most of the countries and the majority of the world's population have not even reached, or have only just reached, the capitalist stage of development. We stated this in section six of our theses, but P. Kievsky, because of lack of attention, or inability to think, did "not notice" that we included this section for a definite purpose, namely, to refute caricature distortions of Marxism. *Only* the advanced countries of Western Europe and North America have matured for socialism, and in Engels's letter to Kautsky (*Sbornik Sotsial-Demokrata)* Kievsky will find a concrete illustration of the real and not merely promised "*idea*" that to dream of the "united action of the proletarians of *all* countries" means postponing socialism to the Greek calends, i.e., for ever.[21]

Socialism will be achieved by the united action of the proletarians, not of all, but of a minority of countries, those that have reached the *advanced* capitalist stage of development. The cause of Kievsky's error lies in failure to understand that. In *these* advanced countries (England, France, Germany, etc.) the national problem was solved long ago; national unity outlived its purpose long ago; *objectively,* there are no "general national tasks" to be accomplished. Hence, only in these countries is it possible *now* to "blow up" national unity and establish class unity.

The *un*developed countries are a different matter. They embrace the whole of Eastern Europe and all the colonies and semi-colonies and are dealt with in section six of the theses (second- and third-type countries). In those areas, as a rule, there *still* exist oppressed and capitalistically undeveloped nations. *Objectively,* these nations still have general national tasks to accomplish, namely, *democratic* tasks, the tasks of *overthrowing foreign oppression.*

Engels cited India as an example of such nations, stating that she might perform a revolution against victorious socialism, for Engels was remote from the preposterous imperialist Economism which imagines that having achieved victory in the advanced countries, the proletariat will "automatically", without definite *democratic* measures, abolish national oppression everywhere. The victorious proletariat will reorganise the countries in which it has triumphed. That cannot be done all at once; nor, indeed, can the bourgeoisie be "vanquished" all at once. We deliberately emphasised this in our theses, and Kievsky has again failed to stop and think *why* we stressed this point in connection with the national question.

While the proletariat of the advanced countries is overthrowing the bourgeoisie and repelling its attempts at counter-revolution, the undeveloped and oppressed nations do not just wait, do not cease to exist, do not disappear. If they take advantage even of such a bourgeois imperialist crisis as the war of 1915-16—a minor crisis compared with social revolution—to rise in revolt (the colonies, Ireland), there can be no doubt that they will all the more readily take advantage of the *great crisis* of civil war in the advanced countries to rise in revolt.

The social revolution can come only in the form of an epoch in which are combined civil war by the proletariat against the bourgeoisie in the advanced countries and a *whole series* of democratic and revolutionary movements, including the national liberation movement, in the undeveloped, backward and oppressed nations.

Why? Because capitalism develops unevenly, and objective reality gives us highly developed capitalist nations side by side with a number of economically slightly developed, or totally undeveloped, nations. P. Kievsky has absolutely failed to analyse the *objective* conditions of social revolution from the standpoint of the economic maturity of various countries. His reproach that we "invent" instances in which to apply self-determination is therefore an attempt to lay the blame at the wrong door.

With a zeal worthy of a better cause, Kievsky repeatedly quotes Marx and Engels to the effect that "one must not invent things out of his own head, but use his head to discover in the existing material conditions" the means that will free humanity of social evils. When I read those oft-repeated quotations I cannot help recalling the late and unlamented Economists who just as tediously. . . harped on their "new discovery" that capitalism had triumphed in Russia. Kievsky wants to "smite" us with these quotations: he claims that we invent out of our own heads the conditions for applying self-determination in the epoch of imperialism! But we find the following "incautious admission" in his own article:

"The very fact we are *opposed* [author's italics] to defence of the fatherland shows most clearly that we will actively resist suppression of a national uprising, for we shall thereby be combating imperialism, our mortal enemy" (Chapter II, §r).

To criticise an author, to *answer* him, one has to quote in full at least the main propositions of his article. But in all of Kievsky's propositions you will find that every sentence contains two or three errors or illogicalities that distort Marxism!

1) He is unaware that a national uprising is *also* "defence of the fatherland"! A little thought, however, will make it perfectly clear that this is so, since *every* "nation in revolt" "defends" itself, its language, its territory, its fatherland, against the oppressor nation.

All national oppression calls forth the resistance of the *broad masses* of the people; and the resistance of a nationally oppressed population always *tends* to national revolt. Not infrequently (notably in Austria and Russia) we find the bourgeoisie of the oppressed nations *talking* of national revolt, while in practice it enters into reactionary compacts with the bourgeoisie of the oppressor nation behind the backs of, *and against,* its own people. In such cases the criticism of revolutionary Marxists should be directed not against the national movement, but against its degradation, vulgarisation, against the tendency to reduce it to a petty squabble. Incidentally, very many Austrian and Russian Social-Democrats overlook this and in their *legitimate* hatred of the petty, vulgar and sordid national squabbles—disputes and scuffles over the question, for instance, of which language shall have precedence in two-language street signs—refuse to support the national struggle. We shall not "support" a republican farce in, say, the principality of Monaco, or the "republican" adventurism of "generals" in the small states of South America or some Pacific island. But that does not mean it would be permissible to abandon the republican slogan for serious democratic and socialist movements. We should, and do, ridicule the sordid national squabbles and haggling in Russia and Austria. But that does not mean that it would be permissible to deny support to a national uprising or a serious popular struggle against national oppression.

2) If national uprisings are impossible in the "imperialist era", Kievsky has no right to speak of them. If they are possible, *all* his fine-spun talk about "monism" and our "inventing" examples of self-determination under imperialism, etc., etc., falls to pieces. Kievsky defeats his own arguments.

If "we" "actively resist suppression" of a "national uprising"—a case which P. Kievsky "himself" considers possible—what does this mean?

It means that the *action* is twofold, or "dualistic", to employ the philosophical term as incorrectly as our author does: (a) first, it is the "action" of the nationally oppressed proletariat and peasantry *jointly* with the nationally oppressed bourgeoisie *against* the oppressor nation; (b) second, it is the "action" of the proletariat, or of its class-conscious section, in the oppressor nation *against* the bourgeoisie of that nation and all the elements that follow it.

The innumerable phrases against a "national bloc", national "illusions", the "poison" of nationalism, against "fanning national hatred" and the like, to which P. Kievsky resorts, prove to be meaningless. For when he advises the proletariat of the oppressor countries (which, be it remembered, he regards as a serious force) "actively to resist suppression of a national uprising", he thereby *fans* national hatred and *supports* the establishment of a "bloc with the bourgeoisie" by the workers of the oppressed nations.

3) If national uprisings are possible under imperialism, so are national wars. There is no material political diffe-

rence between the two. Military historians are perfectly right when they put rebellions in the same category as wars. Kievsky has unwittingly refuted not only himself, but also Junius[22] and the *Internationale* group, who deny the *possibility* of national wars under imperialism. And this denial is the only conceivable theoretical ground for denying self-determination of nations under imperialism.

4) For what is a "national" uprising? It is an uprising aimed at the achievement of *political* independence of the oppressed nation, i.e., the establishment of a *separate* national state.

If the proletariat of the oppressor nation is a serious force (in the imperialist era, as our author rightly assumes), does not its determination "actively to resist suppression of a national uprising" *imply assistance* in creating a separate national state? Of course it does.

Though he denies the "achievability" of self-determination, our brave author now argues that the class-conscious proletariat of the advanced countries must *assist* in achieving this "unachievable" goal!

5) *Why* must "we" "actively resist" suppression of a national uprising? P. Kievsky advances only one reason: ". . . we shall thereby be combating imperialism, our mortal enemy." All the *strength* of this argument lies in the *strong* word "mortal". And this is in keeping with his penchant for strong words instead of strong arguments—high-sounding phrases like "driving a stake into the quivering body of the bourgeoisie" and similar Alexinsky flourishes.

But this Kievsky argument is *wrong*. Imperialism is as much our "mortal" enemy as is capitalism. That is so. No Marxist will forget, however, that capitalism is progressive compared with feudalism, and that imperialism is progressive compared with pre-monopoly capitalism. Hence, it is *not* every struggle against imperialism that we should support. We will *not* support a struggle of the reactionary classes against imperialism; we will *not* support an uprising of the reactionary classes against imperialism and capitalism.

Consequently, once the author admits the need to support an uprising of an oppressed nation ("actively resisting" suppression means supporting the uprising), he also admits that a national uprising is *progressive*, that the establishment of a separate and new state, of new frontiers, etc., resulting from a successful uprising, is *progressive*.

In *none* of his political arguments is the author consistent!

The Irish Rebellion of 1916,[23] which took place after our theses had appeared in No. 2 of *Vorbote*, proved, incidentally, that it was not idle to speak of the possibility of national uprisings *even in Europe*.

6. The Other Political Issues Raised and Distorted by P. Kievsky

Liberation of the colonies, we stated in our theses, means self-determination of nations. Europeans often forget that colonial peoples *too* are nations, but to tolerate this "forgetfulness" is to tolerate chauvinism.

P. Kievsky "objects":

> In the pure type of colonies, "there is *no* proletariat in the proper sense of the term" (end of §r, Chapter II). "For whom, then, is the 'self-determination' slogan meant? For the colonial bourgeoisie? For the fellahs? For the peasants? Certainly not. It is absurd for *socialists* [Kievsky's italics] to demand self-determination for the colonies, for it is absurd in general to advance the slogans of a workers' party for countries where there are no workers."

P. Kievsky's anger and his denunciation of our view as "absurd" notwithstanding, we make bold to submit that his arguments are erroneous. Only the late and unlamented Economists believed that the "slogans of workers' party" are issued *only* for workers.* No, these slogans are issued for the whole of the labouring population, for the entire people. The democratic part of our programme—Kievsky has given no thought to its significance "in general"—is addressed specifically to the whole people and that is why in it we speak of the "people".**

* P. Kievsky would do well to reread what A. Martynov and Co. wrote in 1899-1901. He would find many of his "own" arguments there.

** Some curious opponents of "self-determination of nations" try to refute our views with the argument that "nations" are divided into classes! Our customary reply to these caricature Marxists is that the democratic part of our programme speaks of "government by the people".

The colonial and semi-colonial nations, we said, account for 1,000 million people, and P. Kievsky has not taken the trouble to refute that concrete statement. Of these 1,000 million, more than 700 million (China, India, Persia, Egypt) live in countries where *there are* workers. But even with regard to colonial countries where there are no workers, only slave-owners and slaves, etc., the demand for "self-determination", far from being *absurd,* is *obligatory* for every Marxist. And if he gave the matter a little thought, Kievsky would probably realise this, and also that "self-determination" is always advanced "for" *two* nations: the oppressed and the *oppressing.*

Another of Kievsky's "objections":

> "For that reason we limit ourselves, in respect to the colonies, to a negative slogan, i.e., to the demand socialists present to their governments—'get out of the colonies!' Unachievable within the framework of capitalism, this demand serves to intensify the struggle against imperialism, but does not contradict the trend of development, for a socialist society will not possess colonies."

The author's inability, or reluctance, to give the slightest thought to the theoretical contents of political slogans is simply amazing! Are we to believe that the use of a propaganda phrase instead of a theoretically precise political term alters matters? To say "get out of the colonies" is to evade a theoretical analysis and hide behind propaganda phrases! For every one of our Party propagandists, in referring to the Ukraine, Poland, Finland, etc., is fully entitled to demand of the tsarist government ("his own government"): "get out of Finland", etc. However, the intelligent propagandist will understand that we must not advance either positive or negative slogans for the sole purpose of "intensifying" the struggle. Only men of the Alexinsky type could insist that the "negative" slogan "get out of the Black-Hundred Duma" was justified by the desire to "intensify" the struggle against a certain evil.

Intensification of the struggle is an empty phrase of the subjectivists, who forget the Marxist requirement that every slogan be justified by a precise analysis of *economic* realities, the *political* situation and the *political* significance of the slogan. It is embarrassing to have to drive this home, but what can one do?

We know the Alexinsky habit of cutting short a theoretical discussion of a theoretical question by propaganda outcries. It is a bad habit. The slogan "get out of the colonies" has one and only one political and economic content: freedom of secession for the colonial nations, freedom to establish a separate state! If, as P. Kievsky believes, the *general* laws of imperialism prevent the self-determination of nations and make it a utopia, illusion, etc., etc., then how can one, without stopping to think, make an exception from these general laws for *most* of the nations of the world? Obviously, P. Kievsky's "theory" is a caricature of theory.

Commodity production and capitalism, and the connecting threads of finance capital, exist in the vast majority of colonial countries. How, then, can we urge the imperialist countries, their governments, to "get out of the colonies" if, *from the standpoint* of commodity production, capitalism and imperialism, this is an "unscientific" and "utopian" demand, "refuted" *even* by Lensch, Cunow[24] and the rest?

There is not even a shadow of *thought* in the author's argumentation!

He has given no thought to the fact that liberation of the colonies is "unrealisable" *only* in the sense of being "unrealisable without a series of revolutions". He has given no thought to the fact that it is realisable *in conjunction with* a socialist revolution in Europe. He has given no thought to the fact that a "socialist society will not possess" *not only* colonies, but subject nations *in general.* He has given no thought to the fact that, on the question under discussion, there is *no* economic or political difference between Russia's "possession" of Poland or Turkestan. He has given no thought to the fact that a "socialist society" will wish to "get out of the colonies" *only* in the sense of granting them the free *right* to secede, but definitely *not* in the sense of *recommending secession.*

And for this differentiation between the right to secede and the recommendation to secede, P. Kievsky condemns us as "jugglers", and to "scientifically substantiate" that verdict in the eyes of the workers, he writes:

"What is a worker to think when he asks a propagandist how the proletariat should regard *samostiinost* [political independence for the

Ukraine], and gets this answer: socialists are working for the right to secede, but their propaganda is against secession?"

I believe I can give a fairly accurate reply to that question, namely: every sensible worker will *think* that Kievsky is *not capable of thinking*.

Every sensible worker will "think": here we have P. Kievsky telling us workers to shout "get out of the colonies". In other words, we Great-Russian workers must demand from our government that it get out of Mongolia, Turkestan, Persia; English workers must demand that the English Government get out of Egypt, India, Persia, etc. But does this mean that *we* proletarians *wish* to separate ourselves from the Egyptian workers and fellahs, from the Mongolian, Turkestan or Indian workers and peasants? Does it mean that *we* advise the labouring masses of the colonies to "separate" from the class-conscious European proletariat? Nothing of the kind. Now, as always, we stand and shall continue to stand for the closest association and merging of the class-conscious workers of the advanced countries with the workers, peasants and slaves of *all* the oppressed countries.. We have always advised and shall continue to advise all the oppressed classes in all the oppressed countries, the colonies included *not* to separate from us, but to form the closest possible ties and merge with us.

We demand from our governments that they quit the colonies, or, to put it in precise political terms rather than in agitational outcries—that they *grant* the colonies full *freedom* of secession, the genuine *right to self-determination,* and we ourselves are sure to implement this right, and grant this freedom, as soon as we capture power. We demand this from existing governments, and will *do* this when we are the government, *not* in order to "recommend" secession, but, on the contrary, in order to facilitate and accelerate the *democratic* association and merging of nations. We shall exert every effort to foster association and merger with the Mongolians, Persians, Indians, Egyptians. We believe it is our duty and *in our interest* to do this, for otherwise socialism in Europe will *not be secure*. We shall endeavour to render these nations, more backward and oppressed than we are, "disinterested cultural assistance", to borrow the happy expression of the Polish Social-Democrats. In other words, we will help them pass to the use of machinery, to the lightening of labour, to democracy, to socialism.

If we demand freedom of secession for the Mongolians, Persians, Egyptians and *all* other oppressed and unequal nations without exception, we do so not because *we favour secession,* but *only* because we stand for *free, voluntary* association and merging as distinct from forcible association. That is the *only* reason!

And in this respect the *only* difference between the Mongolian or Egyptian peasants and workers and their Polish or Finnish counterparts is, in our view, that the latter are more developed, more experienced politically than the Great Russians, more economically prepared, etc., and for that reason will in all likelihood *very soon* convince their peoples that it is unwise to extend their present legitimate hatred of the Great Russians, for their role of hangman, to the *socialist* workers and to a socialist Russia. They will convince them that economic expediency and internationalist and democratic instinct and consciousness demand the earliest association of all nations and their merging in a socialist society. And since the Poles and Finns are highly cultured people, they will, in all probability, very soon come to see the correctness of this attitude, and the possible secession of Poland and Finland after the triumph of socialism will therefore be only of short duration. The incomparably less cultured fellahs, Mongolians and Persians might secede for a longer period, but we shall try to shorten it by disinterested cultural assistance as indicated above.

There is *no* other difference in our attitude to the Poles and Mongolians, nor can there be. There is *no* "contradiction", nor can there be, between our propaganda of freedom of secession and our firm resolve to implement that freedom when *we* are the government, and our propaganda of association and merging of nations. That is what, we feel sure, every sensible worker, every genuine socialist and internationalist will "think" of our controversy with P. Kievsky.*

* Evidently Kievsky simply *repeated* the slogan "get out of the colonies", advanced by certain German and Dutch Marxists, without

Running through the article is Kievsky's basic doubt: why advocate and, when we are in power, implement the freedom of nations to *secede,* considering that the trend of development is towards the *merging* of nations? For the same reason—we reply—that we advocate and, when in power, will implement the dictatorship of the proletariat, though the entire trend of development is towards abolition of coercive domination of one part of society over another. Dictatorship is domination of one part of society over the rest of society, and domination, moreover, that rests directly on coercion. Dictatorship of the proletariat, the only consistently revolutionary class, is necessary to overthrow the bourgeoisie and repel its attempts at counter-revolution. The question of proletarian dictatorship is of such overriding importance that he who denies the need for such dictatorship, or recognises it only in words, cannot be a member of the Social-Democratic Party. However, it cannot be denied that in individual cases, by way of exception, for instance, in some small country after the social revolution has been accomplished in a neighbouring big country, peaceful surrender of power by the bourgeoisie is *possible,* if it is convinced that resistance is hopeless and if it prefers to save its skin. It is much more likely, of course, that even in small states socialism will *not* be achieved without civil war, and for that reason the *only* programme of international Social-Democracy must be recognition of civil war, though violence is, of

---

considering not only its theoretical content and implications, but also the specific features of Russia. It is pardonable—to a certain extent—for a Dutch or German Marxist to confine himself to the slogan "get out of the colonies". For, first, the *typical* form of national oppression, in the case of most *West*-European countries, is oppression of the colonies, and, second, the very term "colony" has an especially clear, graphic and vital meaning for West-European countries.

But what of Russia? Its peculiarity lies precisely in the fact that the difference between "*our*" "colonies" and "our" oppressed nations is not clear, not concrete and not vitally felt!

For a Marxist writing in, say, German it might be pardonable to overlook *this* peculiarity of Russia; for Kievsky it is unpardonable. The sheer absurdity of trying to discover some serious difference between oppressed nations and colonies in the case of Russia should be especially clear to a Russian socialist who wants not simply to *repeat*, but to *think*.

course, alien to our ideals. The same, *mutatis mutandis* (with the *necessary* alterations), is applicable to nations. We favour their merger, but *now* there can be no transition from forcible merger and annexation to voluntary merger without freedom of secession. We recognise—and quite rightly—the predominance of the economic factor, but to interpret it *à la* Kievsky is to make a caricature of Marxism. Even the trusts and banks of modern imperialism, though inevitable everywhere as part of developed capitalism, differ in their concrete aspects from country to country. There is a still greater difference, despite homogeneity in essentials, between political forms in the advanced imperialist countries—America, England, France, Germany. The same variety will manifest itself also in the path mankind will follow from the imperialism of today to the socialist revolution of tomorrow. All nations will arrive at socialism—this is inevitable, but all will do so in not exactly the same way, each will contribute something of its own to some form of democracy, to some variety of the dictatorship of the proletariat, to the varying rate of socialist transformations in the different aspects of social life. There is nothing more primitive from the viewpoint of theory, or more ridiculous from that of practice, than to paint, "in the name of historical materialism", *this* aspect of the future in a monotonous grey. The result will be nothing more than Suzdal daubing.[25] And even if reality were to show that *prior* to the first victory of the socialist proletariat only 1/500 of the nations now oppressed will win emancipation and secede, that *prior* to the final victory of the socialist proletariat the world over (i.e., during all the vicissitudes of the socialist revolution) also only 1/500 of the oppressed nations will secede for a very short time—*even* in that event we would be correct, both from the theoretical and practical political standpoint, in advising the workers, already now, not to permit into their Social-Democratic parties those socialists of the oppressor nations who do not recognise and do not advocate freedom of secession for *all* oppressed nations. For the fact is that we do not know, and cannot know, how many of the oppressed nations will in practice require secession in order to contribute something of their own to the different *forms* of democracy, the different *forms* of transition to socialism. And that the negation of freedom of secession now is theoretically false from beginning to end and in practice amounts to servility to the chauvinists of the oppressing nations—this we know, sec and feel daily.

"We emphasise," P. Kievsky writes in a footnote to the passage quoted above, "that we fully support the demand 'against forcible annexation'. . . ."

But he makes no reply, not even by a single word, to our perfectly clear statement that this "demand" is tantamount to recognising self-determination, that there can be no correct definition of the concept "annexation" unless it is seen in context with self-determination. Presumably Kievsky believes that in a discussion it is enough to present one's arguments and demands without any supporting evidence!

He continues: ". . .We fully accept, in their *negative* formulation, a number of demands that tend to sharpen proletarian consciousness against imperialism, but there is absolutely no possibility of working out corresponding *positive* formulations on the basis of the existing system. Against war, yes, but not for a democratic peace. . . ."

Wrong—wrong from the first word to the last. Kievsky has read our resolution on "Pacifism and the Peace Slogan" (in the pamphlet *Socialism and War*, pp. 44-45) and even approved it, I believe. But obviously he did not understand it. We are *for* a democratic peace, only we warn the workers against the deception that such a peace is possible under the present, bourgeois governments "without a series of revolutions", as the resolution points out. We denounced as a deception of the workers the "abstract" advocacy of peace, i. e., one that does *not* take into account the real class nature, or, specifically, the imperialist nature of the *present* governments in the belligerent countries. We definitely stated in the *Sotsial-Demokrat* (No. 47) theses that if the revolution places our Party in power during the present war, it will immediately propose a democratic peace to all the warring countries.

Yet, anxious to convince himself and others that he is opposed "only" to self-determination and not to democracy in general, Kievsky ends up by asserting that we are "not for a democratic peace". Curious logic!

There is no need to dwell on all the other examples he cites, and no sense in wasting space on refuting them, for they are on the same level of naive and fallacious logic and can only make the reader smile. There is not, nor can there be, such a thing as a "negative" Social-Democratic slogan that serves only to "sharpen proletarian consciousness against imperialism" without at the same time offering a positive answer to the question of *how* Social-Democracy will solve the problem when it assumes power. A "negative" slogan unconnected with a definite positive solution will not "sharpen", but dull consciousness, for such a slogan is a hollow phrase, mere shouting, meaningless declamation.

P. Kievsky does not understand the difference between "negative" slogans that stigmatise *political* evils and *economic* evils. The difference lies in the fact that certain economic evils are part of capitalism as such, whatever the political superstructure, and that it is *impossible* to eliminate them economically without eliminating capitalism itself. Not a single instance can be cited to disprove this. On the other hand, political evils represent a departure from democracy which, economically, is fully possible "on the basis of the existing system", i. e., capitalism, and by way of exception is being implemented under capitalism—certain aspects in one country, other aspects in another. Again, what the author fails to understand is precisely the fundamental conditions necessary for the implementation of democracy in general!

The same applies to the question of divorce. The reader will recall that it was first posed by Rosa Luxemburg in the discussion on the *national* question. She expressed the perfectly justified opinion that if we uphold autonomy within a state (for a definite region, area, etc.), we must, as centralist Social-Democrats, insist that all major national issues—and *divorce* legislation is one of them—should come within the jurisdiction of the central government and central parliament. This example clearly demonstrates that one cannot be a democrat and socialist without demanding full freedom of divorce now, because the lack of such freedom is additional oppression of the oppressed sex—though it should not be difficult to realise that recognition of the *freedom* to leave one's husband is not an *invitation* to all wives to do so!

P. Kievsky "objects":

> "What would this right [of divorce] be like if in *such* cases [when the wife *wants* to leave the husband] she could *not* exercise her right? Or if its exercise depended on the will of *third* parties, or worse still, on the will of claimants to her affections? Would we advocate the proclamation of *such* a right? Of course not!"

That objection reveals complete failure to understand the relation between democracy *in general* and capitalism. The conditions that make it impossible for the oppressed classes to "exercise" their democratic rights are not the exception under capitalism; they are typical of the system. In most cases the right of divorce will remain unrealisable under capitalism, for the oppressed sex is subjugated economically. No matter how much democracy there is under capitalism, the woman remains a "domestic slave", a slave locked up in the bedroom, nursery, kitchen. The right to elect their "own" people's judges, officials, school-teachers, jurymen, etc., is likewise in most cases unrealisable under capitalism precisely because of the economic subjection of the workers and peasants. The same applies to the democratic republic: our programme defines it as "government by the people", though all Social-Democrats know perfectly well that under capitalism, even in the most democratic republic, there is bound to be bribery of officials by the bourgeoisie and an alliance of stock exchange and the government.

Only those who cannot think straight or have no knowledge of Marxism will conclude: so there is no point in having a republic, no point in freedom of divorce, no point in democracy, no point in self-determination of nations! But Marxists know that democracy does *not* abolish class oppression. It only makes the class struggle more direct, wider, more open and pronounced, and that is what we need. The fuller the freedom of divorce, the clearer will women see that the source of their "domestic slavery" is capitalism, not lack of rights. The more democratic the system of government, the clearer will the workers see that the root evil is capitalism, not lack of rights. The fuller national equality (and it is *not* complete without freedom of secession), the clearer will the workers of the oppressed nations see that the cause of their oppression is capitalism, not lack of rights, etc.

It must be said again and again: It is embarrassing to have to drive home the ABC of Marxism, but what is one to do if Kievsky does not know it?

He discusses divorce in much the same way as one of the secretaries of the Organising Committee abroad, Semkovsky,[26] discussed it, if I remember rightly, in the Paris *Golos*. His line of reasoning was that freedom of divorce is not, it is true, an invitation to all wives to leave their husbands, but if it is proved that all other husbands are better than yours, madame, then it amounts to one and the same thing!!

In taking that line of argument Semkovsky forgot that crank thinking is not a violation of socialist or democratic principles. If Semkovsky were to tell a woman that all other husbands were better than hers, no one would regard this as violation of democratic principles. At most people would say: There are bound to be big cranks in a big party! But if Semkovsky were to take it into his head to defend as a democrat a person who opposed freedom of divorce and appealed to the courts, the police or the church to prevent his wife leaving him, we feel sure that *even* most of Semkovsky's colleagues on the Secretariat Abroad, though they are sorry socialists, would refuse to support him!

Both Semkovsky and Kievsky, in their "discussion" of divorce, fail to understand the issue and avoid its substance, namely, that under capitalism the right of divorce, as *all* other democratic rights without exception, is conditional, restricted, formal, narrow and extremely difficult of realisation. Yet no self-respecting Social-Democrat will consider anyone opposing the right of divorce a democrat, let alone a socialist. That is the crux of the matter. *All* "democracy" consists in the proclamation and realisation of "rights" which under capitalism are realisable only to a very small degree and only relatively. But without the proclamation of these rights, without a struggle to introduce them now, immediately, without training the masses in the spirit of this struggle, socialism is *impossible*.

Having failed to understand that, Kievsky bypasses the central question, that belongs to his special subject, namely, *how* will we Social-Democrats abolish national oppression? He shunts the question aside with phrases about the world being "drenched in blood", etc. (though this has no bearing on the matter under discussion). This leaves only one single argument: the socialist revolution will solve everything! Or, the argument sometimes advanced by people who share his views: self-determination is impossible under capitalism and superfluous under socialism.

From the theoretical standpoint that view is nonsensical; from the practical political standpoint it is chauvinistic. It fails to appreciate the significance of democracy. For socialism is impossible without democracy because: (1) the proletariat cannot perform the socialist revolution unless it prepares for it by the struggle for democracy; (2) victorious socialism cannot consolidate its victory and bring humanity to the withering away of the state without implementing full democracy. To claim that self-determination is superfluous under socialism is therefore just as nonsensical and just as hopelessly confusing as to claim that democracy is superfluous under socialism.

Self-determination is *no more* impossible under capitalism, and *just* as superfluous under socialism, as democracy generally.

The economic revolution will create the necessary prerequisites for eliminating *all* types of political oppression. Precisely for that reason it is illogical and incorrect to reduce everything to the economic revolution, for the question is: *how* to eliminate national oppression? It cannot be eliminated without an economic revolution. That is incontestable. But to *limit* ourselves to this is to lapse into absurd and wretched imperialist Economism.

We must carry out national *equality;* proclaim, formulate and implement equal "rights" for all nations. *Everyone* agrees with that save, perhaps, P. Kievsky. But this poses a question which Kievsky avoids: is not negation of the *right* to form a national state negation of equality?

Of course it is. And consistent, i. e., socialist, democrats proclaim, formulate and will implement this right, without which there is no path to complete, voluntary rapprochement and merging of nations.

7. Conclusion. Alexinsky Methods

We have analysed only a fraction of P. Kievsky's arguments. To analyse *all* of them would require an article five times the length of this one, for there is not a single correct view in the whole of what Kievsky has to say. What is *correct*—if there are no mistakes in the figures—is the footnote data on banks. All the rest is an impossible tangle of confusion peppered with phrases like "driving a stake into the quivering body", "we shall not only judge the conquering heroes, but condemn them to death and elimination", the "new world will be born in agonising convulsions", "the question will not be one of granting charters and rights, nor of proclaiming the freedom of the nations, but of establishing genuinely free relationships, destroying age-old slavery and social oppression in general, and national oppression in particular", and so on and so forth.

These phrases are, at one and the same time, the cover and expression of two things: first, their underlying "idea" is *imperialist Economism*, which is just as ugly a caricature of Marxism, and just as complete a misinterpretation of the relationship between socialism and democracy, as was the late and unlamented Economism of 1894-1902.

Second, we have in these phrases a repetition of Alexinsky methods. This should be especially emphasised, for a whole section of Kievsky's article (Chapter II, §f, "The Special Position of the Jews") is based *exclusively* on these methods.

At the 1907 London Congress[27] the Bolsheviks would dissociate themselves from Alexinsky when, in reply to theoretical arguments, he would pose as an agitator and resort to high-falutin, but entirely irrelevant, phrases against one or another type of exploitation and oppression. "He's begun his shouting again," our delegates would say. And the "shouting" did not do Alexinsky any good.

There is the same kind of "shouting" in Kievsky's article. He has no reply to the theoretical questions and arguments expounded in the theses. Instead, he poses as an agitator and begins shouting about the oppression of the Jews, though every thinking person will realise that his shouting, and the Jewish question in general, have no relation whatever to the subject under discussion.

Alexinsky methods can lead to no good.

Written August-October 1916
First published in the magazine
Zvezda Nos. 1 and 2, 1924

Collected Works, Vol 23, pp. 28-76

Notes

1 *Economism*—an opportunist trend in the Russian Social-Democratic movement at the turn of the century. The Economists were opposed to Social-Democrats taking part in the political struggle and maintained that the working class should confine itself to the economic struggle for better working conditions, higher wages, etc. They advanced the erroneous un-Marxist thesis that "politics always follow obediently in the wake of economics". They made a fetish of the spontaneity of the working-class movement and denied the leading role of the party and the importance of Marxist theory to the working-class movement.

Lenin sharply criticised Economism in *What Is To Be Done?* and other works, and also in his articles published in *Iskra*. The revolutionary Social-Democrats' ideological struggle against the Economists ended in the smashing defeat of the latter. By the Second Congress of the R.S.D.L.P. (1903) the Economists had lost all their influence among the workers. p. 7

2 *Iskrists*—supporters of the first all-Russian underground Marxist newspaper *Iskra* founded by Lenin abroad in December 1900 and illegally circulated in Russia. The newspaper was instrumental in the ideological consolidation of the Russian Social-Democrats and paved the way for the unification of isolated local organisations into a revolutionary Marxist party. p. 7

[3] *Narodism*—an ideological and political trend in Russia that arose in the 1870s. Narodniks were petty-bourgeois democrats whose programme included the abolition of the autocracy and the transfer of all land to the peasants. They denied the leading role of the working class in the revolutionary movement, erroneously maintaining that socialist revolution could be accomplished by small peasant proprietors. They regarded the peasant commune, that survival of feudalism and serfdom in the Russian countryside, as a germ of socialism. The socialism they preached was utopian, as it was not based on actual social development. p. 7

[4] This refers to the boycott of the so-called Bulygin Duma.

Frightened by the sweep of the revolution, the tsarist government adopted a law on August 6(19), 1905 instituting the State Duma; the bill was prepared by Minister of the Interior Bulygin. It was to be a consultative, not a legislative, body. The workers and peasants remained practically without a vote.

The Bolsheviks urged the workers and all working people to actively boycott the Duma and prepare for an armed uprising. In the meantime the revolutionary tide was rising. Strikes and demonstrations under the slogan "Down with the autocracy!" swept through Russia. In October 1905 an all-Russia political strike took place and in December an armed uprising began in Moscow. The revolution swept away the Bulygin Duma which was never convened. p. 7

[5] Lenin has in mind otzovism, an opportunist trend among a section of Bolsheviks that arose after the 1905-07 revolution. The otzovists (Bogdanov, Alexinsky and others) proposed tactics that were inapplicable in the conditions of the defeat of the revolution and the onset of reaction. They demanded the recall (hence their name, from the Russian word "*otozvat*", to recall) of the Social-Democratic deputies from the Duma and the renunciation of the work in legal trade union, co-operative and other workers' organisations. They were against combining legal and illegal forms of activity, maintaining that the Party should engage in illegal activity only. The implementation of their slogans would have led to the weakening of the Party's ties with the masses and made the Party itself a sectarian organisation incapable of rallying the forces for a new revolutionary upsurge. Lenin and an overwhelming majority of the Bolsheviks gave a fitting rebuff to the otzovists. p. 7

[6] Lenin means P. Kievsky's (G. A. Pyatakov[45]) article "The Proletariat and the 'Right of Nations to Self-Determination' in the Epoch of Finance Capital".

Lenin's article "A Caricature of Marxism and Imperialist Economism" and Kievsky's article were to be published in *Sbornik Sotsial-Demokrata* No. 3. The magazine, however, did not appear at the time and the articles were not printed. p. 8

[7] Lenin refers to the collapse of the Second International and the split in the international socialist movement in 1914. When the

First World War began, most of the leaders of the socialist parties affiliated to the Second International betrayed socialism and sided with their governments, supporting the imperialist war. The Russian Bolsheviks with Lenin at their head and the German Left Social-Democrats Karl Liebknecht, Rosa Luxemburg and others, and some groups in other socialist parties remained loyal to the principles of internationalism and called on the workers of their countries to fight their imperialist governments and the imperialist war. p. 8

8 Clause 9 of the Party Programme adopted at the Second Congress of the R.S.D.L.P. in 1903 contained the demand for the right to self-determination for all nations. p. 8

9 The reference is to the conference of the R.S.D.L.P. sections abroad which met in Berne from February 27 to March 4, 1915. It was called on Lenin's initiative and played the role of a Bolshevik party conference, since it was impossible to hold an all-Russia conference during the war. At the conference Lenin represented the Central Committee and the Central Organ *(Sotsial-Demokrat)*, directed the work of the conference and spoke on the main item on the agenda "The War and the Tasks of the Party". The Conference adopted resolutions on the war which had been drawn up by Lenin. p. 9

10 *Guesde, Jules* (1845-1922)—one of the leaders of the socialist movement in France. On the outbreak of the war he took a social-chauvinist stand and entered the bourgeois cabinet. p. 12

11 *Plekhanov, G. V.* (1856-1918)—prominent figure in the Russian and international working-class movement; was the first to popularise Marxism in Russia. During the First World War he was social-chauvinist. p. 13

12 *Kautsky, Karl* (1854-1938)—one of leaders of the German Social-Democrats and of the Second International, ideologist of centrism. During the First World War he defended social-chauvinism under the cover of internationalist phraseology. p. 14

13 *The Internationale group* was established by the German Left Social-Democrats Karl Liebknecht, Rosa Luxemburg, Franz Mehring, Clara Zetkin and others soon after the outbreak of the First World War. The group fought against German imperialism and exposed the Social-Democratic leaders who had sided with the imperialists. The German government severely persecuted the group for its revolutionary activity. Rosa Luxemburg and other members of the group held erroneous views on a number of theoretical and political questions. V. I. Lenin criticised their mistakes in his works "The Junius Pamphlet", "A Caricature of Marxism and Imperialist Economism" and elsewhere. In January 1916 the group began to be called the Spartacus group and later on Spartacus League. In December 1918 the Spartacists founded the Communist Party of Germany. p. 16

[14] This refers to Lenin's theses "The Socialist Revolution and the Right of Nations to Self-Determination, which he wrote in January-February 1916. The theses were published in the magazine *Vorbote* No. 2 in April 1916 (see V. I. Lenin, *Collected Works*, Vol. 22, pp. 143-56). p. 17

[15] *V. Ilyin*—the pen name of V. I. Lenin. p. 18

[16] See F. Engels, *The Origin of the Family, Private Property and the State*, Ch. IX (Marx and Engels, *Selected Works*, Vol. 3, Moscow, 1970, p. 329. p. 25

[17] *The Erfurt Programme*—the programme of the German Social-Democratic Party, adopted at the congress of the Party in Erfurt in 1891. p. 29

[18] *Martov, Y. O.* (1873-1923)—Russian Social-Democrat, one of the Menshevik leaders. p. 34

[19] *Dühring, Eugen* (1833-1921)—German philosopher and economist, ideologist of the petty bourgeoisie. F. Engels criticised Dühring's views in his work *Anti-Dühring. Herr Eugen Dühring's Revolution in Science.* p. 34

[20] *Fracy*—the Right wing of the Polish Socialist Party (PPS), a reformist nationalist party founded in 1892. p. 37

[21] See F. Engels's letter to K. Kautsky of September 12, 1882. p. 38

[22] *Junius*—the pen name of Rosa Luxemburg, a prominent figure in the German and Polish working-class movement. p. 42

[23] In April 1916 the Irish revolted against the British domination to win independence. The Dublin workers, the petty bourgeoisie of the city and the Irish Volunteers (the organisation led by Left-wing leaders of the Irish national liberation movement) seized power in the city and proclaimed a republic. Simultaneously armed action was taken in other towns and counties.

The British Government sent troops and artillery units to suppress the uprising. Dublin was shelled from a British warship. The heroic struggle in Dublin against heavy odds lasted for a week. The British Government defeated the insurgents and drowned the movement in blood. Several thousand people were thrown into prisons and the leaders of the insurrection were executed. p. 43

[24] *Lensch, Paul* (1873-1926) and *Cunow, Heinrich* (1862-1936)—extreme Right German Social-Democrats, apologists of imperialism, who opposed the granting of independence to the colonies. p. 45

[25] *Suzdal daubing*—generally, crude botching. The expression refers to the crudely painted icons for which Suzdal uyezd in Russia was notorious. p. 49

[26] *Organising Committee* (O. C.)—the leading centre of the Mensheviks.

Semkovsky, S. Y. (b. 1882)—Russian Social-Democrat, Menshevik. p. 53

[27] Reference is to the Fifth Congress of the R.S.D.L.P. which was held in London from April 30 to May 19 (May 13-June 1), 1907. p. 55

CPSIA information can be obtained at www.ICGtesting.com
Printed in the USA
LVOW06s1323240815

451307LV00001B/35/P